Sacajawea

The Windcatcher

©™

~ Foreword ~

This concept book is about Sacajawea, The Windcatcher, and how she came to our world with the force of a whirlwind...

She moved through time and space, over mighty rivers and magnificent mountains, determined to reach the Great Water with her prayers. She is a spirit who is driven to share her message of love.

Sacajawea's first encounter with us was to wake us up, to infiltrate our lives, to show us something greater than ourselves. We have been walking this journey for many years, with our own stories to tell, and she has been patient to guide us.

We believe Sacajawea, The Windcatcher, is a story that will change the world, for it is a catalyst for what we seek.

Thank you for embracing her light and walking this path with us.

ONWARD! We have no fear.

Jane L. Fitzpatrick

She stays a mystery through the Ages.
A young Shoshone girl, stolen away and
traded to a Frenchman for a gun.

Yet, her mark on history remains.
In the adventure that will birth a nation,
she sees a way home.

But Destiny has another plan...

See the journey through her eyes.

4

Sacajawea waits, she prays, she wonders, she believes. Through the Ages, her destiny is made real. From her deepest, darkest cave, we will learn about the power of Light.

At 12 years old, Sacajawea's Spirit Chief cleanses her for a transcendent journey.

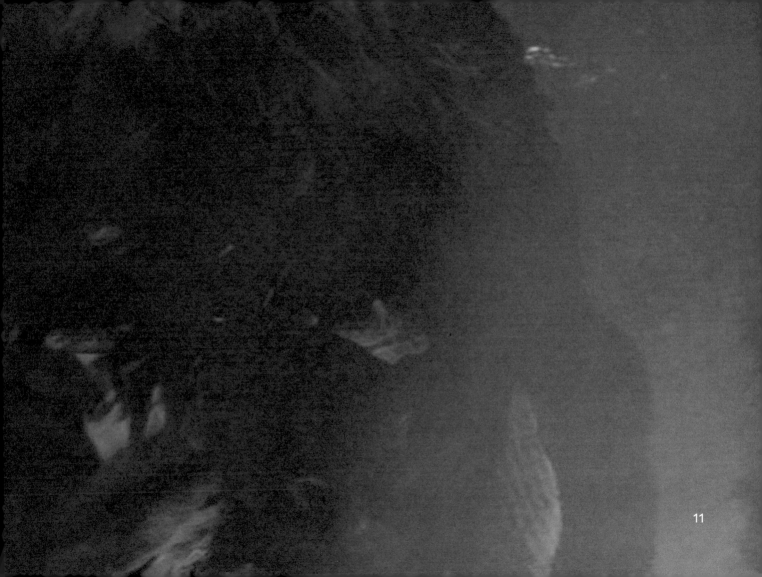

11

After Sacajawea's moontime celebration,
she is kidnapped by Hidatsa warriors.

WHITE EAGLE
Digital Character Concept Artwork

12

Through the clouds, Sacajawea reaches out to Spirit.
She knows there is a way home...

...because Spirit is reaching back.

Soldiers arrive at the Hidatsa village
needing Shoshone horses to cross the
mountains. Though pregnant,
Sacajawea will guide them to her People
in the spring.

Digital Character Concept Sketches

20

Journal Sketching

With her fingertips she holds the wind, a symbol of air calls to her spirit.

Sacajawea carries mankind on her back... it is her Calling as a mother now, and as a warrior woman.

23

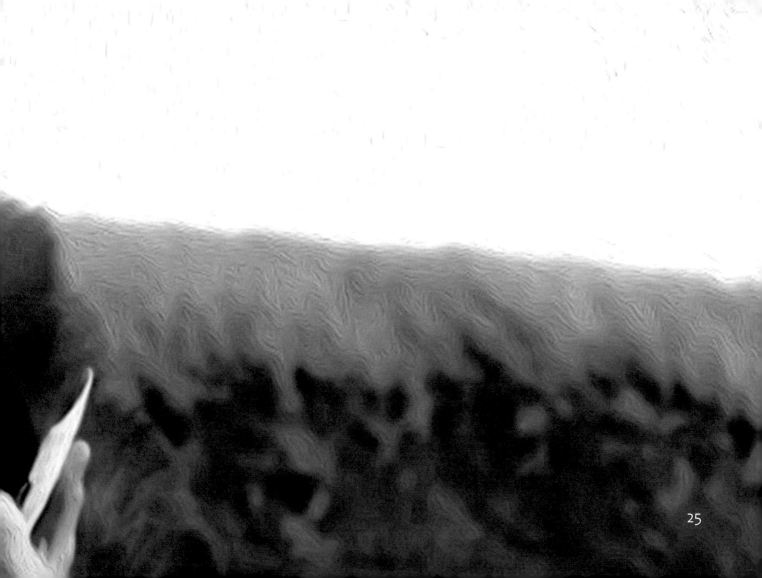

Sacajawea is overjoyed to find her People - but so sad she cannot stay, for she and her son belong to the white man. In her sorrow, she prays for a sign from Spirit. Then her chief shows her a new path and a greater purpose.

Still heartsick, Sacajawea meets a Nez Perce Shaman who tells her, "Your spirit is weak. It waits with another."

WATKUWEIS
Digital Character Concept Artwork

Downriver, Flathead warriors rush the camp... a Shoshone slave boy is with them. He thinks Sacajawea is his mother, and she knows her spirit is waiting with this child.

BROWN BEAR
Digital Character Concept Artwork

During the winter at Fort Clatsop, a warrior with white skin and red hair leads Sacajawea to the Great Water.

JACK RAMSEY
Digital Character Concept Artwork

38

With the force of a whirlwind, Sacajawea soars over mighty rivers and magnificent mountains. It is her path to stand at the Great Water and send her prayers to every shore.

Sacajawea is awakening the world to something greater than self!

The sun hangs just above the horizon - its glorious array spans across the Heavens. It is the gloaming, and the sounds of raptors' wings meet our ears. We are here to awaken in this magical moment when an eagle feather floats quietly from the sky. It is a gift! We reach out to receive its message...

...and we remember a woman.

41

We are called to tell the untold story of
Sacajawea and to share this truth:
It is our spirit, and our spiritual health,
that carries us in life, and after life,
through a transparent belief in the
Infinite Oneness of Love.

Sacajawea, The Windcatcher

Vol. I - THE PATH

Published by Spirit Wind Films & Media, Portland, OR

info@sacajaweathemovie.com
www.sacajaweathemovie.com
www.warriorwomanspirit.com

Sacajawea, The Windcatcher, is based on a true story and inspired by the journals of the Lewis & Clark Expedition.

Author & Photography, Jane L. Fitzpatrick
Concept Artwork & Graphic Design, Marcia K. Moore
Sacajawea Logo Feather Design, Shawna N. Fitzpatrick

Sacagawea

The Windcatcher

©™

JANE L. FITZPATRICK, Writer – As a writer, my passion is to bring the stories of history to life. I have been writing for more than 30 years, including creative and business writing, website content and blogging. The epic screenplay, *Sacajawea, The Windcatcher*, is a story that touched me deeply. It required me to change, to get out-of-the-way and awaken. I was humbled when the script was selected and nominated for BEST PERIOD PIECE by the 2013 Action On Film International Film Festival. At this time, I am writing the story into a novel by the same name, to accompany the film's distribution. It has also been a dream to write stories for children. Therefore, I completed a family-centered spec script entitled *Kimama's Wings*, and a pre-teen chapter book, *Crabtree*, which is being developed for film. One of my greatest joys was to collaborate with my daughter and granddaughter for the illustrations, and publish the children's book, *The Grass Maiden, Sacajawea*, based on my research from the feature film. It was important to create a story to share Sacajawea's message of love with children. Other projects related to Sacajawea are in development as well as a miniseries based on her son's life.

MARCIA K. MOORE, Concept Artist, Traditional – Digital Artist – As an artist, I am compelled to reconstruct history using my traditional art tools and modern software technology. It is my hope that artistically reconstructing (repatriating) the past will help us understand lost history. A responsibility....dedicated to future generations. Utilizing my art skills and tools has helped assist independent researchers around the world with forensic reconstruction, giving the ancients a face to aid in the understanding of physical anomalies. Through this body of work, I am reconstructing the past, revealing personalities in the flesh that may guide us to a greater understanding of our lost history.

Sacajawea, The Windcatcher,
is based on a true story and
inspired by the journals of the
Lewis & Clark Expedition.

Made in United States
Troutdale, OR
07/12/2023

11195818R00031